ELLIOTT CARTER

CALL

fanfare for two trumpets and horn

HENDON MUSIC

BOOSEY & HAWKES

DISTRIBUTED BY

HAL•LEONARD®
CORPORATION

7777 W. BLUEMOUND RD. P.O. BOX 13819 MILWAUKEE, WI 53213

www.boosey.com
www.halleonard.com

for Frank Scheffer

CALL

Elliott Carter
(2003)

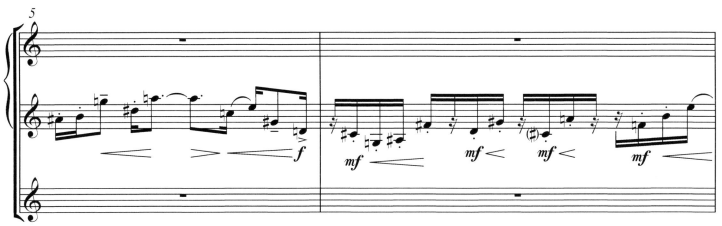

979-0-051-10530-4

Printed in U.S.A.

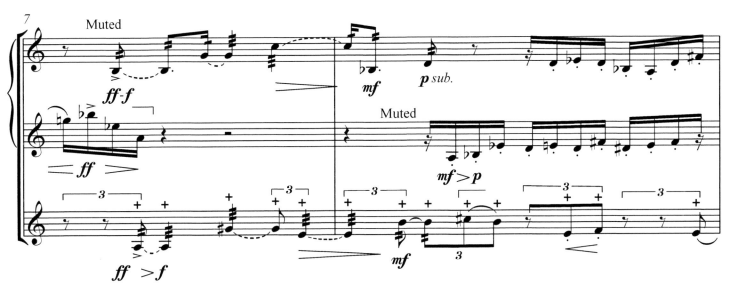

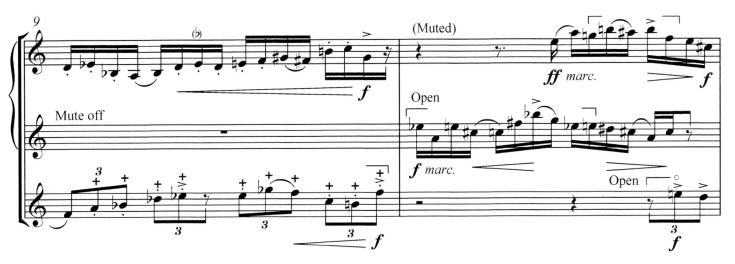

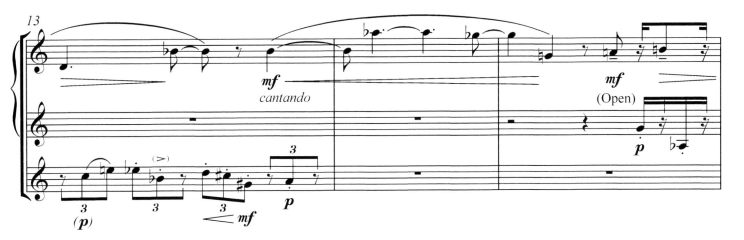

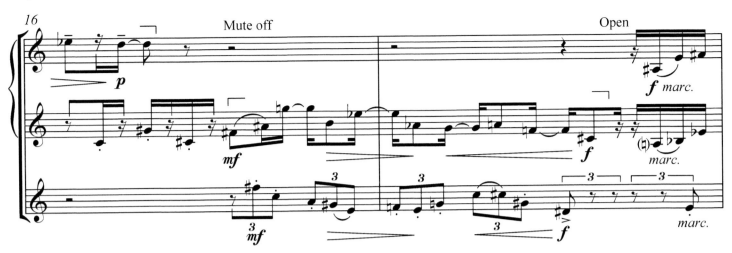

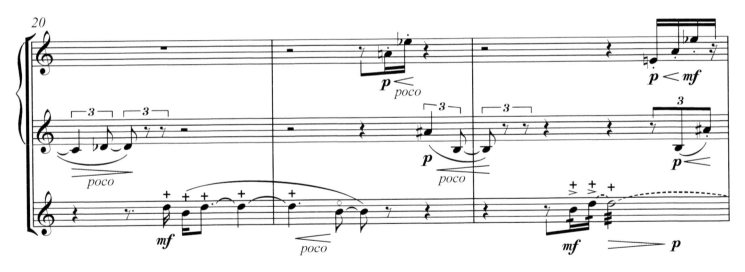

ELLIOTT CARTER

CALL

fanfare for two trumpets and horn

HENDON MUSIC

7777 W. BLUEMOUND RD. P.O. BOX 13819 MILWAUKEE, WI 53213

www.boosey.com
www.halleonard.com

HORN in F

for Frank Scheffer

CALL

Elliott Carter
(2003)

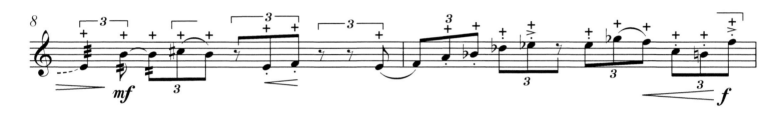

979-0-051-10530-4

Printed in U.S.A.

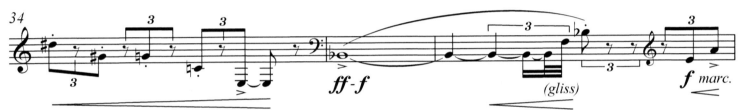

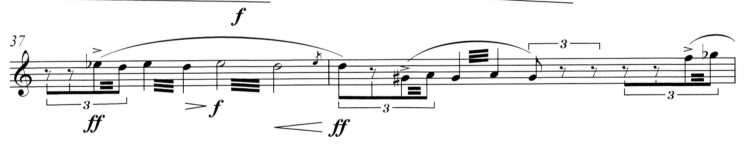

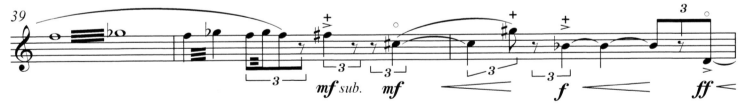

ELLIOTT CARTER

CALL

fanfare for two trumpets and horn

HENDON MUSIC

DISTRIBUTED BY

HAL•LEONARD®
CORPORATION
7777 W. BLUEMOUND RD. P.O. BOX 13819 MILWAUKEE, WI 53213

www.boosey.com
www.halleonard.com

TRUMPET 1 in C

for Frank Scheffer

CALL

Elliott Carter
(2003)

♩ = 108

ELLIOTT CARTER

CALL

fanfare for two trumpets and horn

HENDON MUSIC

BOOSEY & HAWKES

DISTRIBUTED BY

HAL•LEONARD®
CORPORATION
7777 W. BLUEMOUND RD. P.O. BOX 13819 MILWAUKEE, WI 53213

www.boosey.com
www.halleonard.com

TRUMPET 2 in C

for Frank Scheffer

CALL

Elliott Carter
(2003)

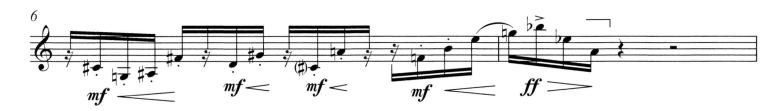

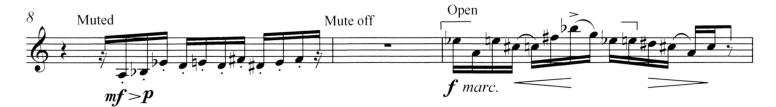

979-0-051-10530-4

Printed in U.S.A.

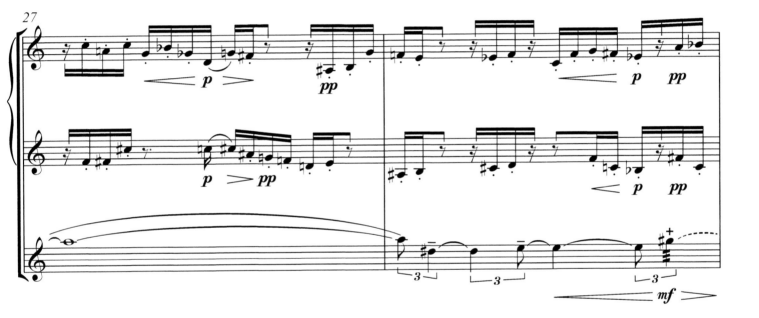

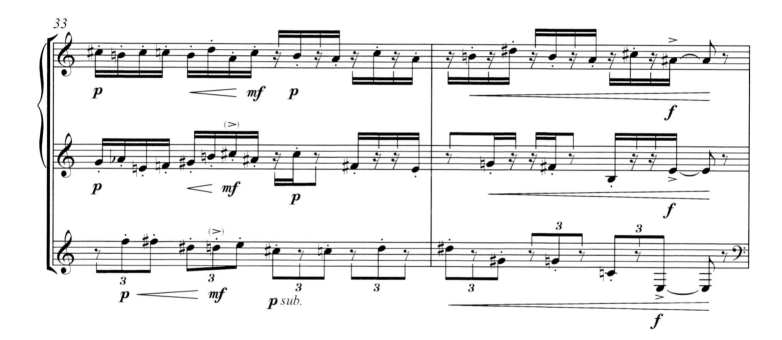

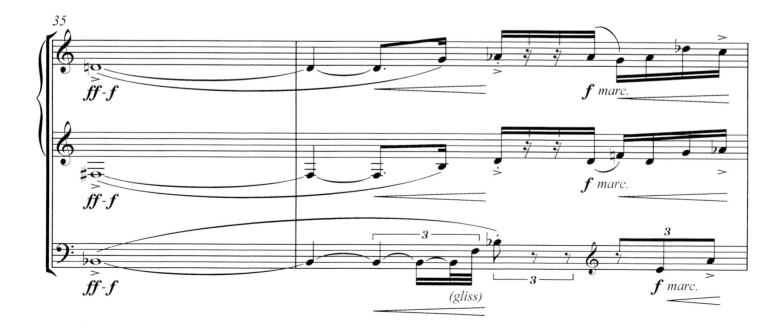

N.Y.C. 10/06/03